COULD DO BETTER

COULD DO BETTER

Norman McGreevy

CONSTABLE • LONDON

Constable & Robinson Ltd
3 The Lanchesters
162 Fulham Palace Road
London W6 9ER
www.constablerobinson.com

First published in the UK by Constable,
an imprint of Constable & Robinson Ltd, 2010

A copy of the British Library Cataloguing in
Publication data is available from the British Library

ISBN: 978-1-84901-359-8

Printed and bound in the EU

1 3 5 7 9 10 8 6 4 2

CONTENTS

Dear Reader,

You may remember that, towards the end of the previous book, this almost Zen-like sentence, lifted from a schoolchild's essay, pops up: 'A gelding is a stallion who has his tonsils taken out so he would have more time to himself.'

That's it. But what on earth did it mean? There seemed to be *something* in there, some insight, a truth, a place where we could immerse ourselves in hours of deep and profound meditation. We don't know where it came from. It made no sense at all but for some reason it made us laugh.

And that is what this second compilation is about. Laughter. The kind of laughter that comes from the natural and uncontrived humour of schoolchildren, for whom words are just rubbery, many-sided globs of thought that can be wrestled and pummeled into all sorts of hilarious shapes. From another essay writer who felt – 'Losing my dog was the final straw in the camel's pack' – to the religious essayist who believed that – 'When Mary heard she was the mother of Jesus, she sang the Magna-Carta' – to the historically unlikely – 'Joan of Arc was condomed to death'.

In this new volume, I hope I have chosen the right howlers for you. If they remind you of some good ones you had forgotten; if they add a few more to your repertoire; above all, if they provide a few smiles and belly-laughs, this book will have achieved the purpose for which it was compiled.

Norman McGreevy

Essays

Big flies were hoovering all round the room.

Romeo and Juliet tell each other how much
they are in love in the baloney scene.

She draped her posterior over a grubby stool.

Both his legs were cut off, and both his hands,
and most of his brains were hanging through
the side of his head; and he was lying on his
bed – crying.

I took out a book to read and settled down to
read, but soon put it down because I couldn't
read.

Big flies were hoovering all round the room

All walks and no play makes Jack a doll boy.

Her hair is always hanging about her moon-shaped face with horn-rimmed spectacles.

Swollen dead bodies were taken to the doctor for cross-examination.

I was given a blanket and some coffee, but I could not drink them.

To prevent head colds, use an agonizer to spray into your nose until it drops down into your throat.

People were carrying on in the quiet way to which they had been accustomed since time immoral.

A cigarette hung out of the corner of her eye.

I summed up my ailments to be double pneumonia and a weak heart. I hauled myself to my feet and began to walk again to try and keep warm and to take my mind off my stomach.

We were trapped in a blazing car, but luckily enough a river was passing by.

His mother, being immortal, had died.

The equator is a menagerie lion running around the Earth through Africa.

Some people can tell the time by looking at the sun, but I have never been able to make out the numbers.

If I pass in front of a person I have to say 'Excise me!'

My nose was stagnant, and my ears weren't in the best of health.

As she went through her wardrobe she found a scorpion in her drawers. She rose quickly.

He didn't walk through the door – he crawled in; this was a precaution he always took.

One of the advantages of living in Austria is that one can hear the Matterhorn being blown.

All brutes are imperfect animals, man alone is the perfect beast.

Her appearance is made more beautiful by her wasp waist which protrudes out on the hips and breast.

There are four kinds of food – tined, jared, caned and raped.

I quickly glanced at the grandfather clock in my
waistcoat pocket

I quickly glanced at the grandfather clock in my waistcoat pocket.

Many protesters have tried Gandhi's method of non-active activity.

I was nervous, but at last I gathered up my guts and spoke to him.

Clowns tie their trousers with string which, when it is pulled, shows a hair-raising scene.

When the amplifiers are turned up full-blast, everybody in the village almost evacuates.

It was about dusky when I aroused from my slumble.

Old people look back on the past, young people look back on the future.

I can't live without you she burst out in his arms. Clear drops – the jewels of her starry eyes – flowed down and soaked his shirt. He felt them, and they pierced his heart – to leave a deep cut.

Was I to be abandoned sine die in such ternicious envirolment? With this intimating thought I doozed off.

II

My wife has the baby, and you will never see it again; there was no name or signature written on the bottom.

At the age of seventeen I have finally been accepted by my family.

Slowly the upper deck became occupied with travellers who wished to relieve themselves.

All your responses must be oral, OK? What school did you go to? 'Oral'.

After several years his business began to flush.

Pavlov studied the salvation of dogs.

I used to leave my class and walk all over the school interfering with the children of the higher forms. Sometimes when I was not in school they came to see me.

The primary aim of education should be to equip a man to earn his own living. This is so important that it should be repeated. The primary aim of education should be to equip a man to earn his own living. Indeed, it cannot be said too often that the primary aim of education should be to equip a man to earn his own living.

Miscellany

When father passed away they burned his ashes and brought them home in a urinal.

Vesuvius is a volcano and if you will climb up to the top you will see the creator smoking.

One of the knights took him at his word and stabbed the Archbishop in the cathedral.

An octopus is a person who hopes for the best.

Magnesium is the best thing for babies. It will stop almost anything.

A Protestant is a woman who gets her living through immoral life.

Newspapers are useful for reporting calamities such as deaths, marriages, etc.

You shake milk in a big stirrer machine to make it homicidal.

Isaac Newton passed the law of gravity.

The Indian squabs carried porpoises on their back.

A momentum is what you give a person when they are leaving.

Trigonometry is when a lady marries three men at the same time.

Michael Angelo painted the selling of the cistern chapel.

An anachronism is a thing that a man puts in writing in the past before it has taken place in the future.

Hamlet had an edible complex.

Trigonometry is when a lady marries three men at the same time

Caviar is the eggs of a surgeon.

The dog ran across the lawn, emitting whelps all the way.

Marconi is used to make delicious puddings.

Etiquette is the noise you make when you sneeze.

Europe was disrupted by the fast paste of change. Industrialization was precipitating in England.

Barbarians are things put into bicycles to make them run smoothly.

Politicians turn to and fro in their perplexity, weaving and unweaving their combinations.

A virgin forest is a forest where the hand of man has never set foot.

Q: In a democratic society, how important are elections?

A: Very important. Sex can only happen when a male gets an election.

In a sand storm the camels put their heads in the sand
and let the sand find its own destination

Q: What are steroids?
A: Things for keeping carpets still on the stairs.

In a sand storm the camels put their heads in the sand and let the sand find its own destination.

The spinal column is a long bunch of bones.

The head sits on the top and you sit on the bottom.

A scout obeys all to whom obedience is due and respects all duly constipated authorities.

By self pollination, the farmer may get a flock
of long-haired sheep.

An epitaph is a horse with the head of a man.
The feminine of manager is managerie.

An incomplete thought is called a frays.

A monologue is a dialogue for one person.

An aristocrat is a man who does somersaults
on the stage.

Glaziers are common, they move about a metre a day in Switzerland.

A metaphor is a thing you shout through.

Crematorium is French for a dairy.

Terra cotta is stuff squeezed out of little insects and used to turn puddings red.

Transparent means something you can see through. For instance, a keyhole.

It was moonlight and the air was soft and putrid.

Rhetoric is a form of arithmetic.

A connoisseur is a man who stands outside the hotel.

The masculine of heroine is kipper.

The plural of spouse is spice.

The Last Post is always sounded by the burglars at funerals.

The plural of spouse is spice

A barrister is a thing put up in the street to keep the crowds back.

Iron was discovered because someone smelt it.

An oboe is an American tramp.

Parsimony is money left by your father.

A refugee keeps order at a football match.

The embalmed body of an Egyptian is called a dummy.

The future of 'I give' is 'You take'.

The two kinds of book printed are friction and non-friction.

Being between the Scylla and Charybdis means that whichever way you go, you are going to get got.

'Bring out your dead' is what the judge said when a prisoner was brought for trial from the cells.

Tarzan is a short name for the American flag. It's full name is Tarzan Stripes.

A prospectus is a man who finds gold

The round towers are tall towers built in memory of the dead, but for what purpose is not known.

Petroleum is what you cover floors with.

He did not give a name to this picture, but called it 'A unanimous picture of an old lady.'

A prospectus is a man who finds gold.

A monologue is a conversation between two people, such as husband and wife.

Hiatus: breath that wants seeing to.

Before being captain of his ship he had worked as an amiable seaman.

In some places they have smoking aloud.

What qualifications are required for a special constable? Any respectable man is illegible.

Pandemonium not only reigned, it poured.

Catharsisis a psychological means of stopping a catarrh. It illustrates the influence of mind over body.

Celibacy is a disease of the brain.

The Dauphin was a rare fish that used to inhabit the Arctic Circle in the middle ages.

Chivalry is the act of a man who gives his seat to a lady in a public convenience.

Mussolini is a sort of material used for ladies' stockings.

An epidemic is a needle the doctor used to put medicine in your arm.

Etiquette is little things you do that you don't
want to do.

Genius is an infinite capacity for picking
brains.

An heir is when anybody dies you get what
is left.

A dynamo is a machine that makes dynamite
and other explosions.

A prodigal is the son of a priest.

A Senator is half horse and half man.

A dynamo is a machine that makes dynamite
and other explosions

A sinecure is a disease without a cure.

I intend to pass all my testes.

A man is an animal split half way up and walks on the split end.

A caucus is a dead animal.

An eavesdropper is a kind of bird.

A Home is where you live with your loved ones, and a House is a big mansion on a hill with plenty of trouble.

My friend and I are very thrusting with each other.

We spent the day rumping on the sands.

He had a special cabaret built in his room to house all his 200 models.

A pedagogue is an animal with large ears.

An imbecile is a germ floating around in the air which anybody is liable to catch.

Lumbago is a mineral used in making lead pencils.

Mastication is what the Italians do with their hands when they talk English.

A millennium is something like a centenial, only it has more legs.

Mistletoe is a man who hates all mankind.

It is bad manners to break your bread and roll in your soup.

They lent him money so that he could do drinking and thus relieve himself.

The people were very angry and gnashed at him with his teeth.

The South of Scotland abounds in green pastors.

Running is a great sport, and I thank God for exposing me to the track team.

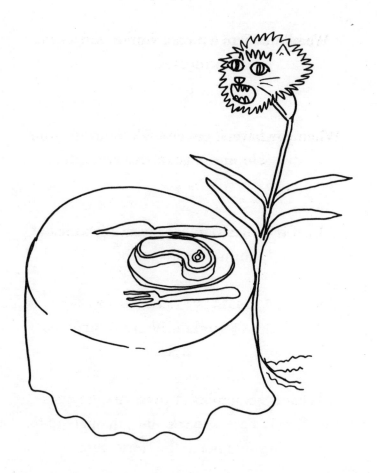

A cat is a carnation because he eats meat

We sat down to a picnic dinner of fricken chicasee.

When you haven't got enough iodine in your blood you get a glacier.

A cat is a carnation because he eats meat.

The parcel couldn't be found as a we taken it for granite.

What is a microbe? A robe that the mics wear.

A fissure is a man who sell fish.

What is the longest day in the Southern Hemisphere? Sunday.

A cyclone is a man riding a bicycle.

A blood vessel is a man's lifeboat.

When there are no fresh vegetables, you can always get canned.

Quotations and Translations

Honi soit qui mal y pense.
He may be honest who thinks badly.

))

Hors de combat.
War Horse.

))

Coup de grace.
A lawnmower.

))

Joie de vivre.
Whisky.

))

Tete a tete.
Having tea twice.

Tete a tete. Having tea twice.

Hors d'oeuvre.
Out of work.

Ave Domine.
Lord, I am a bird.

The masculine of belle.
Stomach.

E.g.
Egg sample.

Volte-face.
Made a horrible face.

Sotto voce.
In a drunken voice.

᛭᛭

Etc.
It is a sign used to make believe you know
more than you do.

Religion

Christians were condemned to death in large groups. They entered the arena to face wild lions singing hymns of praise in the name of the Father, the Son, and in-the-Hole-He-Goes.

Martin Luther was nailed to the church door at Wittenburg for selling papal indulgences.

Saul was commanded to kill everybody. This he did in a half-hearted fashion as he nailed the King to a tree.

Moses went up on Mount Cyanide to get the Ten Commandments.

Abraham begat Isaac and Isaac begat Jacob and Jacob begat twelve partridges.

Samson slayed the Philistines by pulling down the pillows of the temple.

Moses ate nothing but whales and manner for forty years. He died before he ever reached Canada.

As Isaac grew up he always domineered, so the only thing to do was to turn him into the dessert.

The greatest miracle was when Joseph told his son to stand still and he obeyed him.

Whenever David played to Saul the latter
kept a javelin handy

Whenever David played to Saul the latter kept a javelin handy.

Jesus was born because Mary had an Immaculate Contraption.

If David had one fault it was a slight tendency to adultery.

Little is known of the prophet Elijah, except that he once went for a cruise with a widow.

Before a man could become a monk he had to have his tonsils cut.

A parable is a heavenly story with no earthly meaning.

Sarah was Abraham's half-wife, otherwise mid-wife, sometimes called columbine.

Abraham, after the sacrifice of Isaac, called the place Rio Janeiro.

Acrimony (sometimes called holy) is another name for marriage.

The first five books of the Bible are Genesis, Exodus, Laxatives, Deuteronomy and Numbers.

Adam and Eve were created from an apple tree. One of their children, Cain, asked, 'Am I my brother's son? My punishment is greater than I can bare.'

Noah's wife was called Joan of Ark. He built an ark, which the animals came on to in pears.

Saddam and Gomorrah were twins.

God asked Abraham to sacrifice Isaac on Mount Montezuma.

Esau was a man who wrote fables and sold his copyright for a mess of potash.

Old Testament profits include Moses, Amy, and Confucius, who believed in Fidel Piety.

A Protestant is any one who is not a Catholic. Roman Catholics believe what the Pope speaks, but Protestants can believe what they like.

Martin Luther did not die a natural death, he was excommunicated by a bull.

A martyr is a pile of wood set on fire with a man on top.

David was a fictional character in the Bible who fought with Gilgamesh while wearing a sling.

Jesus cured Peter's mother-in-law when she was sick of a fever, and Peter swore and went out and wept bitterly.

Jacob stole his brother's birthmark.

A deacon is the lowest form of Christian.

Samson was a strong man who was led astray by a Jezebel called Delilah.

The first book in the bible is Guinessis.

Bearing false witness against one's neighbour is when nobody did nothing, and somebody went and told of it.

Deism was the belief that God made the world then stepped in it.

Jesus enunciated the golden rule which says – to do one to others before they do one to you.

He also explained that man does not live by sweat alone.

The first book in the bible is Guinessis

Zacharias was burning insects when he saw an angel.

The locusts were the chief plague. They ate all the first born.

They were God's phropets and epistles.

Jesus was crucified on his way to Calgary. It was a miracle when he rose from the dead and managed to get the tomb stone off the entrance.

The people who followed the Lord were called the twelve decibels.

Noah was the man who danced before the ark,
but first he sent the bird away.

Jacob had a brother called Aseesaw.

The Great Flood was sent because of the large
numbers of dirty people.

John the Baptist was beheaded with the Axe of
the Apostles.

You must love your neighbour even if you hate
him.

If someone slaps you, turn and let him have another knock and the door shall be opened.

Two Jesuits, probably a man and wife, were on the way to Emmaus.

The 'last supper' is the sacrament administered to a dying Catholic.

Who was sorry when the Prodigal Son returned? The fatted calf.

Christianity was introduced into Britain by the Romans in 55 BC.

An Evangelist is one who brings the gossip.

The first and greatest Commandment is hang all the law and the prophets.

Celibacy is the crime a priest commits when he marries.

The bell knolled a knell, and all partakers came to a stand still.

Monasteries were places where monsters were kept.

Four men came out carrying a parable on a bed

Christ came to bring salivation to mankind.

The Pharisees were people who liked to show
off their goodness by praying in synonyms.

Four men came out carrying a parable on
a bed.

There is always a knave in churches to remind
you of sin.

Satan's sin was pride but I thought the really
arrogant one was God.

A martyr is something like a bachelor.

The catacombs were where the early Christians lived when they were put to death by Nero.

And some fell on stony ground and the fowls of the air sprang up and choked them.

The Decalogue is a low-necked frock.

A certain man drew his bow at a venture, but missed and hit Ahab.

Aaron was a good man, who helped Moses with his conjuring tricks.

A passover is a man who goes from bad to worse, like Judas Iscariot.

And he said: 'What shall I do to inherit internal life?'

History

After they defeated Carthage, the Romans brutaly salted the people and razored the city.

The warmth and friendship of the mystery cults atrracted many, who came for the dancing and mutilation.

Shakespeare wrote tragedies, comedies, and hysterectomies, all in Islamic pentameter.

Plato was the teacher of Harris Tottle.

Queen Elizabeth was called the Virgil Queen because she knew Latin.

In 1588 Queen Elizabeth calmed her soldiers during a Spanish attack by telling them that she shared a stomach with her father.

In the Middle Ages King Alfred conquered the Dames.

Egypts rulers were etitled to be known as Faroes. King Toot was one famous Faroe.

Julius Caesar extinguished himself on the battlefields of Gaul.

Sir Francis Drake circumcised the world with a 100-foot clipper.

Kink Nebodresser lived in a hanging garden to please his Hutterite wife.

Charles the First was going to marry the Infanta of Spain. He went to see her, and Shakespeare says he never smiled again.

Henry the Eighth was very pious, and he had a hymn book chained up in every church.

The death of Julius Caesar was foretold by a shower of metaphors.

In the fourteen hundreds most Englishmen were perpendicular.

William the Conqueror was the first of the Mormons.

Until Raleigh brought tobacco back, Elizabeth regarded him as one of her nights.

Julius Caesar was known for his great strength. He threw a bridge across the Rhine.

Henry met Becket on the altar steps and severely massacred him.

The Black Death was spread from port to port by inflected rats. It was then passed on by midgets.

Martin Guerre, a French pesant, did not even seem to care if his wife produced a hare.

Cesar was assassinated on the yikes of March.

The pyramids were large square triangles built in the desert. O'Cyrus, a god who lived in a pyramid, would give you the afterlife if your sole was on straight.

Eyptian mummies were able to live after life through the arts and facts buried with them.

Alexander the Great was born in the absence of his parents.

Martin Guerre, a French pesant, did not even seem to
care if his wife produced a hare

Sparta protested, saying all the cities' fornications in Greece should be dismantled.

No one saw the meteorological rise of the Mycenean ruling class.

When Plato wrote his theory he did so in the form of a diologue which was supposed to have been said by Socrates, another infamous philosopher.

The government in Athens was a democracy. In Sparta it was an allegory.

What was the Age of Pericles? I'm not sure, but I reckon he was about forty.

In his First Meditation Descartes abandons half his body, but to exist he needs a whole mind.

Joan of Arc won her battle because the enemy's wind came across to her. As soon as that happened she knew God was on her side.

Civilization woozed out of the Nile about 1 million BC.

The mother of Achilles dipped him in the River Stynx until he became intolerable.

Hannibal is a well-known music writer.

Hamlet rations out his situation by relieving himself in a long soliloquy.

Souls were believed to spend the 'here, there and after' in Ethiopia.

William the Conqueror landed in 1066 AD. and AD means after dark.

The Greeks were a highly sculptured people, and without them we wouldn't have history.

Arranged marriages required Greek women to accept a kind of mate accompli.

William the Conqueror was thrown from his horse and wounded in the feudal system and died of it.

Lady Macbeth tried to convince Macbeth to kill the King by attacking his manhood.

The scientific method came into use when the Greeks learned never to take things for granite when solving a problem.

Archimedes made the first steamboat and power drill.

King Minoose became the head Cretin of Crete.

The Romans came again 100 years after their
first visit, 90 years before.

Hannabelle crossed the Alps with a herd of
elephints and thus invaded Africa.

Henry the First's son was drowned in the
White Ship, and never smiled agin.

William Tell shot an arrow through an apple
while standing on his son's head.

Romans persecuted Christians by lionizing
them in public stadiums.

A tidal wave of Goths, Hungs, Zulus and others impacted Rome.

The Roman Empire fell through smoking from lead pipes.

When they got to Italy the Australian Goths were tired of plungering and needed to rest.

Edward the Second would have been King of France if his mother had been a man.

After the great feasts, William the First used to entertain the barons by letting off fireworks.

Homer tells us that Greek semen ruled the Agean.

In midevil times most of the people were alliterate.

King Arthur was a person who was washed up when a baby, and Merlin said it should be so, and they proved it.

Sumerian culture began about 3,500 years before Christmas.

Octavian kept the people happy by giving them breaded circuses.

The symbol of Augustine's authority was the cross. He put it everywhere.

Queen Elizabeth was the last of the Roses, and, fearing that Mary Queen of Scots would marry her husband, Sir Walter Raleigh, she beheaded her, and in remorse sent Raleigh to discover America.

The Norman used to put mokes around their castles to protect them from attack.

Henry the Fifth spent all his time with low-down thieves and made life a pleasure.

Martin Luther was on a diet of worms

Martin Luther was on a diet of worms.

By a trick the Greeks enjuiced the Persians to attack.

By the year 1000, people were afraid that an acropolis was lurking around the corner.

The Pilgrim Fathers became a big band of Quackers.

The great wall of China was built to keep out the mongrels.

Roman women built fires in their brassieres.

In the Middle Ages knights fought on horses. This was called jesting.

In 328 BC Rome was invaded by the Gals.

The title 'Defender of the Faith' was given to Henry the Eighth after he was annulled.

The two major religions of Ireland are Catholic and Prostitute.

John Paul Jones became one of America's great nasal heroes.

The invention of the steamboat caused a network of rivers to spring up.

The Romans drove the Pixies over Hadrian's Wall.

The power of the church was based on soul control of the sacer mints.

Monks were assigned to monkeries where they were supposed to live as nuns. Many, however, simply preyed by day and played by night.

Queen Mary had all the Protestants put under the steak.

Henry the Eighth had an abbess on his knee, which made walking difficult.

Margo Polo visited Kukla Kahn who rained in China at the time.

St Patrick abolished all the rats.

Queen Elizabeth the First had a great sporting spirit and she was weaned from her man o' war with difficulty.

It was an age of important inventions and discoveries. Gutenberg invented removable type and the Bible. Another great invention was the circulation of blood.

Henry the Eighth had an abbess on his knee, which
made walking difficult

The South Sea Bubble was a scream for lending money to the government.

Henry the Seventh passed a law saying that no man must have a liver.

Christopher Columbus was a great navigator who discovered America while cursing about the Atlantic.

George the First was the son of Edward the Black Prince or William of Orange.

Richard the Second was murdered in Pontefract Castle, but his fate is unknown.

The people of Vienna used to call their king a dog, but they did not prernounce it the same.

Russia was ruled by a lot of rulers. First by Peter the Great from Pitsburg.

France was torn apart by noble fractions.

Drake knew all about the Armada before he saw it, so he was able to go on bowelling.

Cortez subdued the inhabitants of New Mexico with ease. Small box was killing the natives at a very quick rate. This bothered the Spanish little, for as Catholics they did not believe in God.

The government of England was a limited mockery.

Philip the Second later annoyed the Dutch by speaking to them in Spanish, a language he did not understand.

'Habeas Corpus' was a phrase of the Great Plague and means 'Bring out your dead.'

John Calvin Klein translated the bible into American so the people of Geneva could read it.

Queen Victoria was one of the best reigners. When she died, soldiers fighting in the Boer War left the war to come and see the last of her.

Parliament was a house where men sat and disgusted bills.

Witch hunts erupted in countries such as Germany, England, Scotland and Salem. The victims were usually older post-marsupial women.

Galileo showed that the earth was round and not vice versa. He dropped his balls to prove gravity.

Samuel Morse invented a code for telepathy.

Louis Pastuer discovered a cure for rabbis.

Guerilla warfare means up to their monkey tricks.

The Navy is sometimes called the Senile Service.

Napoleon wanted an heir to inherit his power, but since Josephine was a baroness, she couldn't have any children.

Abraham Lincoln's mother died in infancy. He was born in a log cabin which he built with his own hands.

On the night of 14 April 1865, Lincoln went to the theatre and got shot in his seat.

The first man who went to the Cusades was Robinson Crusoe.

In 1918 more people died from Spanish Fly than from the First World War.

Watchword of the French Revolution 'Liberty, Equality and Infirmity.'

Melba – where Napoleon was imprisoned.

The fate of Bonnie Prince Charlie was sealed at Culloden and he flew to France via Sky.

The cause of the Indian Mutiny was that the Sepoy soldiers before they could use their cartridges had to be greased with the fat of a pig.

One of the causes of the American Revolution was the English put tacks in their tea. Also, the colonists would send their parcels through the post without stamps.

The Boston Tea Party was held at Pearl Harbor.

The Constitution of the United States was adopted to secure domestic hostility, and the people enjoyed the right to keep bare arms.

The battle of Trafalgar was fought at sea, and therefore is sometimes called Waterloo.

Marie Curie won the Noel prize for inventing the radiator.

Thomas Jefferson, a Virgin, and Benjamin Franklin were two singers of the Declaration of Independence.

Queen Victoria was the longest queen.
She sat on a thorn for sixty-three years

An example of imperialism is Rudward Kissinger's poem 'The White Man's Burden'.

Queen Victoria was the longest queen. She sat on a thorn for sixty-three years.

The British First World War Prime Minister was Lord Gorge.

Florence Nightingale never got any sleep for three years because she was continually being needed by the soldiers.

Napoleon fertilized all his life. His only son died by a sphere.

Abraham Lincoln wrote the Gettysburg address while travelling from Washington to Gettysburg on the back of an envelope.

The battle of Trafalgar was fought at sea. It was one of those battles that cannons did better than cavalry.

When Lincoln was President, he wore only a tall silk hat. He said, 'In onion there is strength.'

During the Napolenonic wars, the crowned heads of Europe were tremoling in their shoes.

Cyrus McCormick invented the McCormick raper, which did the work of a hundred men.

Sydney was founded by people who had been executed.

The cause of the great Schism was that the Pope had his head in Rome and his seat in Avignon.

The Pope declared Luther's writings to be hereditary.

Napoleon dispersed the rioters with a whiff of grapefruit.

Frederick William the Electrode fought on both sides in several wars.

The edict of Nantes was a law passed by Louis XIV forbidding all births, marriages, and deaths in France for a period of one year.

Franklin D. Roosevelt was crippled by Polyhole.

The Soviet is what the middle-classes call their napkin.

Caesar was murdered by the Ides of March because they thought he was going to be made king.

Catherine the Great's husband was hung by her supporters.

China has always followed Confusion as a religion.

Darwin's theory of the 'survival of the fetus'.

In March 1936, Hitler sent his troops into the Rainland.

The leader of the Bolsheviks was John Lennon.

The population of China was about 99 per cent Chinese and the other half Manchu.

Very slowly, yet strategically, Hitler acquired divine power.

Stalin sent peasants who had misbehaved to Serbia.

Hitler transformed Germany into a land of blond-eyed, blue-haired super-humans.

As Hitler said, 'You can fool all of the people all of the time and some of the people from time to time.'

The Civil Rights movement in the USA turned around the corner with Martin Luther Junior's famous 'If I had a hammer' speech.

China has so many Chinese that forced birth patrol became required. This is where people are allowed to reproduce no more that one half of them elves.

Cameraship was often stressed in the Hitler Youth.

Japan boomed Pearl Harbor, the main US base in southern California. American sailors watched in shock as the sky filled with Japanese zebras.

Stalin, Roosevelt, Churchill and Trueman were known as the 'Big Three'.

The Nazis hoped to create enough sympathetic rubber and oil to help German re-armament.

The Russian army defended Stalingrad feercely, as the city was named after Lenin.

Hitler had become depressed for some reason and crawled under Berlin. Here he had his wife Evita put to sleep and then shot himself in the bonker.

South Africa followed 'Apart Hide', a policy that separated people by slim colour.

Science and
Nature

A ruminating animal is one that chews
its cubs.

Reproduction is the process by which an orgasm
is made by two or one parent organisms.

Cyanide is so poisonous that one drop of
it on a dog's tongue will kill the strongest
man.

Quinine is the bark of a tree: canine is the bark
of a dog.

Man is the only animal who can strike a light.

When you breath you inspire. When you do not breathe you expire.

Cadavers are dead bodies that have donated themselves to science. This procedure is called gross anatomy.

Cheek cells should be scrapped from the lining of the mouth with a septic stick or a knife or razor blade.

Atoms are made up of protons, electrons and newtons.

Test for a chloride, a sulphate and a night rate.

We tried to dissolve mable in water.

The best thing for a drowned person is to tie their tongue under their chin and make them walk about, or else keep them warm and give them something better than brandy.

The blood vessels are the veins, arteries and artilleries.

Sex and reproduction don't need to go hand in hand.

There are three spaces in the body; the head, chest and trunk, holding respectfully the brain, heart and vowels.

Female mammals have memory glands.

Measurements of the length, breath and mass of the maggot should be made to see how long a maggot took to turn into a pupil.

The best food for babies is oxygen, hydrogen and a little carbon.

The four stages of metamorphosis are egg, lava, pupil, adult.

In the Biology lesson we talked about biol which is produced in the liver.

Earthworms can be recognized by their non-existent hard skeleton.

Earthworms may only see another earthworm every five years because they have no eyes.

After ten days, the stickleback fries hatch.

Some people say we condescended from the apes.

III

The leopard has black spots which look like round soars on its body. Those who catch soars get leprosy.

If conditions are not favourable, bacteria go into a period of adolescence.

All animals were here before mankind. The animals lived peacefully until mankind came along and made roads, houses, hotels and condoms.

If you cross XY and XX chromosones, you get XX (female), YY (male) and XY (undecided).

The moon is a planet just like the earth, only it is even deader.

Pollination is the exchange of pollen from the antler to the stigma.

One of the wonders of modern science is bringing a dead body back to life by artificial insemination.

Incests have six legs.

We used a filter to separate the purities from the impurities.

Intensity of an earthquake is measured on the Bacardi scale.

Climate is caused by the emotion of the earth around the sun.

A grasshopper has three pair of wings – anterior, posterior and bacteria.

The solid wastes are excreted through the retina.

The plains of Siberia are roamed over by the lynx and larynx.

The chief animals of Australia are the
kangaroo, larkspur, boomerang and
peddadillo.

Q: What is meant by 'endangered species'?
A: It is soon to be killed off.

The same thing happens when you add acid to
an alkie.

The mosquito is an insect, but when it bites
anyone it swells up and is very painful.

The female reproductive system: the virgina;
the whom.

The penis becomes erect due to abnormal blood in it.

It is possible to find out the weight of magnesium before being burned.

In the flame test, concentrated acid is used so cation is necessary.

After burning the magnesium, I had a white ass.

We worked it out by a process of illumination.

One mole of a substance contains a number of particles called the avocado number.

We held the crucible with our thongs.

Potatoes are tubas.

Scientists are hypothetical people.

Typhoid fever may be prevented by
fascination.

Freelance eggs are more natural than battery-
produced ones.

If a wound only bleeds very slowly it is venus
bleeding.

A skeleton is a man with his inside out and his outside off.

A vacuum is an empty space where the Pope lives.

Many dead animals of the past changed to fossils while others preferred to be oil.

The cerebral hemispheres are where you would find your morals.

Average means something that hens lay eggs on.

Algebraical symbols are those used when you do not know what you are talking about.

A compass tells a man where he ought to go and always points at the sun.

For asphyxiation, apply artificial respiration until the patient is dead.

Inertia is that which tends to have a uniform motion in a state of rest.

Talc is found on rocks and on babies.

When you look in a mirror the angel of incidence equals the angel of reflection.

When heating aluminium, the end fell off before I felt anything.

We held the crucible with our tongues.

The liquid smelt like nail vanish.

We released the acid onto the marble chips which then went out of the sidearm.

A super-saturated solution is one that holds more than it can hold.

A magnet is a thing you find in a bad apple. Most books now say our sun is a star. But it still knows how to change back into a sun in daytime.

Science is material; religion is immaterial.

Most of atomic physics has got something to do with atoms.

The climate is hottest next to the Creator.

Water is turned into a viper when it gets too hot.

The process of turning steam into water again is called conversation.

Symmetrical means relating to dead bodies.

Methane, a greenhouse gas, comes from the burning of trees and cows.

As the rainforests in the Amazon are shrinking, so are the Indians.

An elephant is a square animal with a tail in front and behind.

One part of an insect is the thorax, which contains the organs of digestion. The latter is not of much use and will soon be discontinued.

The hookworam larva enters the body through the soul.

Male mammals have eternal sexual organs.

My pores are my hands without which I could not write or work.

Food enters the elementary canal at the buckle cavity.

The hyena never attacks anything unless they run away then they just leave them for dead.

When they broke open molecules, they found they were only stuffed with atoms, but when they broke open atoms, they found them stuffed with explosions.

While the earth seems to be knowingly keeping its distance from the sun, it is really only centrificating.

Someday we may discover how to make magnets that can point in any direction.

Q: Name the four seasons.
A: Salt, pepper, mustard and vinegar.

Q: Explain one of the processes by which water
can be made safe to drink.
A: Flirtation makes water safe to drink.
It removes large pollutants like grit, sand
and dead sheep.

Q: What is a planet?
A: A body of earth surrounded by sky.

Q: What happens to your body as you age?
A: When you get old, so do your bowels and
you get intercontinental.

Q: Name the four seasons.
A: Salt, pepper, mustard and vinegar

We say the cause of perfume disappearing is evaporation. Evaporation gets blamed for a lot of things people forget to put the top on.

To most people solutions mean finding the answers. But to chemists solutions are things that are still all mixed up.

In looking at a drop of water under a microscope, we find there are twice as many H's as O's.

Water vapour gets together in a cloud. When it is big enough to be called a drop, it does.

South America has cold summers and hot winters, but somehow they still manage.

I am not sure how clouds get formed. But the clouds know how to do it, and that is the important thing.

A vibration is a motion that can't make up its mind which way it wants to go.

Genetics explain why you look like your father and if you don't why you should.

Some oxygen molecules help fires burn while others help make water, so sometimes it's brother against brother.

Magnet: Something you find crawling all over a dead cat.

Momentum: What you give a person when they are going away.

Before giving a blood transfusion, find out if the blood is affirmative or negative.

The reason the experiment did not work is a complete misery to me!

The pistol of a flower is its only protection against insects.

The alimentary canal is located in the northern part of Indiana.

A permanent set of teeth consists of eight canines, eight cuspids, two molars and eight cuspidors.

A fossil is an extinct animal. The older it is, the more extinct it is.

Q: What is the most common form of contraception?
A: Most people wear a condominium.

Q: What is a seizure?
A: A Roman emperor.

A cuckoo does not lay its own eggs.

The three cavities of the body are the head cavity, the tooth cavity and the abominable cavity.

The cause of dew is through the earth revolving on its own axis and perspiring freely.

For a nosebleed: Put the nose much lower then the body until the heart stops.

For dog bite: Put the dog away for several days. If he has not recovered, then kill it.

Mare Curie did her research at the Sore Buns Institute in France.

Involuntary muscles are not as willing as voluntary ones.

Hot lather comes from volcanoes, when it cools it turns into rocks.

Algebra was the wife of Euclid.

It is a well-known fact that a deceased body harms the mind.

Humans are more intelligent than beasts because the human branes have more convulsions.

It is so hot in some places that people there have to live in other places.

When oxygen is combined with anything, heat is given off. This is known as constipation.

A thermometer is an instrument for raising temperance.

Geometry teaches us to bisex angels.

The theory of evolution was greatly objected to because it made man think.

We believe that the reptiles came from the amphibians by spontaneous generation and study of rocks.

To remove dust from the eye, pull the eye down over the nose.

The disease will spread through areas where the population is higher or more dense. Signs and symptoms of arthritis: Joints all rusty.

Signs and symptoms of arthritis: Joints all rusty

Humans and ruminants both feed on dead organic matter with an alimentary canal.

Ruminants do not need to eat meat and poultry and live on pasteur.

The immune system is easily weekend.

Polo bears are mammals of the arctic regions.

When an animal grows its cells divide and it becomes more intellectual.

Blood platelets gather at the sight of the wound.

High blood pressure causes a cerebral hemisphere in the brain.

Multiple sclerosis causes lack of metal co-ordination.

Lions and giraffes live on the planes of Africa.

The unknown knob on the balance is not really unknown, I just don't know what it is for.

Since 1923, there has been a steady decrease in morality caused by strong eathquakes.

Music

A good orchestra is always ready to play if the conductor steps on the odium.

At one time, singers had to use musicians to accompany them. Since synthesizers came along, singers can now play with themselves.

Contralto is a low sort of music that only ladies sing.

A virtuoso is a musician with real high morals.

Beethoven expired in 1827 and later died from this.

Henry Purcell is a well-known composer few people have ever heard of.

Mandolines are high officials in China.

A fugue is what you get in a room full of people when all the windows and doors are shut.

Aaron Copland is one of your most famous contemporary composers. It is unusual to be contemporary. Most composers do not live until they are dead.

In the last scene of Pagliacci, Canio stabs
Nedda who is the one he really loves. Pretty
soon Silvio also gets stabbed, and they all live
happily ever after.

Music sung by two people at the same time is
called a duel.

When a singer sings, he stirs up the air and
makes it hit any passing eardrums. But if he is
good, he knows how to keep it from hurting.

Pavarotti was at first an Italian. Then someone
heard his voice and said he would go a long
way. And so he went to America.

Music sung by two people at the same time
is called a duel

Probably the most marvellous fugue was the one between the Hatfields and McCoys.

My favourite composer is Opus.

For some reason, they always put a treble clef in front of every line of flute music. You just watch.

A contra-bassoon is like a bassoon, only more so.

Tubas are a bit too much.

It is easy to teach anyone to play the maracas. Just grip the neck and shake him in rhythm.

Just about any animal skin can be stretched over a frame to make a pleasant sound once the animal is removed.

To descant is to pour out the air above the tune.

Three-four time is simply cripple time.

Esipodical form is when one tune goes out while the other comes in.

Silence in music is shown by putting your feet
down on the paddles.

Handel wrote the 'Messiah' and later 'The Lost
Chord'. It is the latter people cannot forget.

The great twelfth-century Notre Dame de
Paris duo – Lenin and Protein.

Another name for kettle drums is timpani. But
I think I will just stick with the first name and
learn it good.

A trumpet is an instrument when it is not an
elephant sound.

The double bass is also called the bass viol, string bass, and bass fiddle. It has so many names because it is so huge.

Cymbals are round, metal CLANGS!

A bassoon looks like nothing I have ever heard.

The main trouble with a French horn is it's too tangled up.

The flute is a skinny-high shape-sounded instrument.

The most dangerous part about playing cymbals is near the nose.

Beethoven wrote music even though he was deaf. He was so deaf he wrote loud music. He took long walks in the forest even when everyone was calling him. I guess he could not hear so good.

Morris dancing is a country survival from times when people were happy.

Most authorities agree that music of antiquity was written long ago.

An octet is a figure with eight sides.

Scales are of two kinds – diatonic and rheumatic.

A chromatic scale is formed entirely of semi-circles.

Syncopation is emphasis on a note that is not in the piece.